D1357651

Shopkins™

Once you shop...You can't stop!

Pedigree®

Published 2015. Pedigree Books Limited, Beech Hill House, Walnut Gardens,
Exeter, Devon EX4 4DH. www.pedigreebooks.com – books@pedigreegroup.co.uk
The Pedigree trademark, email and website addresses, are the sole and exclusive
properties of Pedigree Group Limited, used under licence in this publication.

© MOOSE ENTERPRISE PTY LTD, 2013
29 GRANGE ROAD, CHELTENHAM VIC 3192, AUSTRALIA
www.mooseworld.com.au info@moosetoys.com

CONTENTS

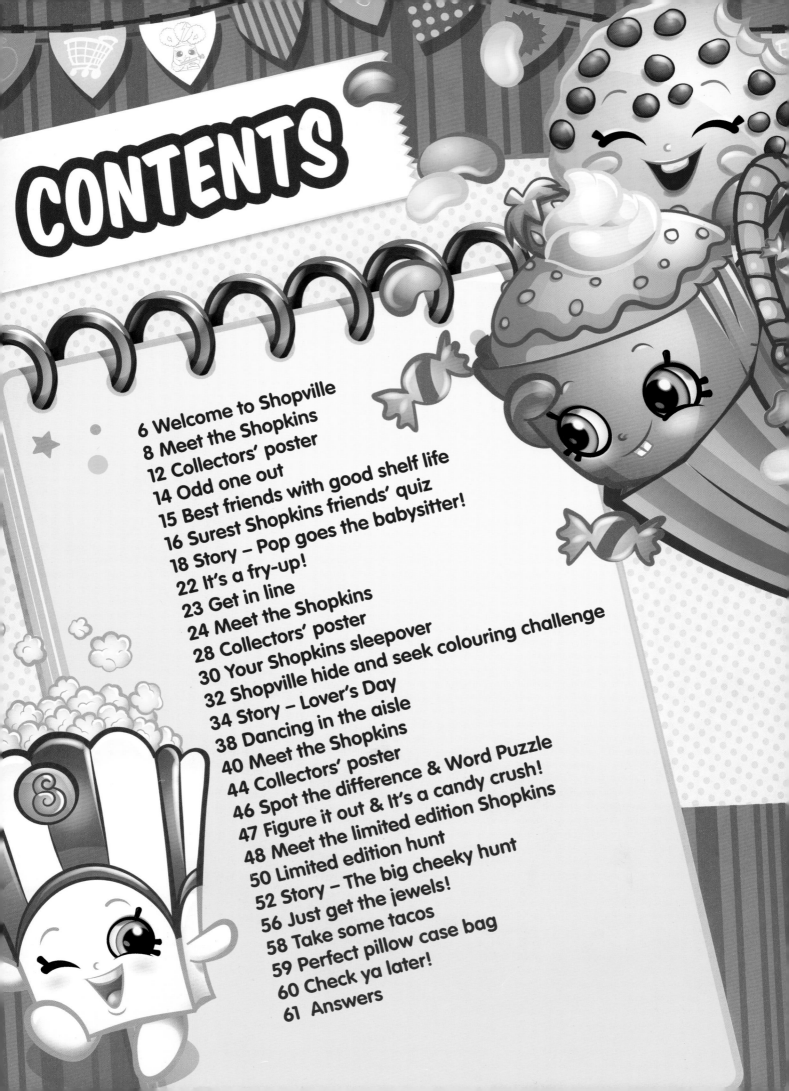

WELCOME TO SHOPVILLE –

It's baskets of fun! Come inside!

There's nowhere quite like Shopville with its bright, cheerful colours and sweet, friendly Shopkins. There are so many treats to put in the trolley, where will you begin? Shop away and start your super-cute Shopkins collection with your BFFs. If you've already started, keep shopping and collect them all.

Your old friends Apple Blossom, Lippy Lips, Kooky Cookie, Strawberry Kiss, Cheeky Chocolate, D'Lish Donut and Chee Zee are all busy inside the Small Mart, and they've got new friends for you to meet and collect.

All you need is one empty shopping trolley and your collector's guide at the ready!

There are hundreds of Shopkins to collect now and the shelves are fully stocked!

Look out for the Exclusive characters which are hidden somewhere on pages throughout this Annual. You know how they love to play hide and seek – there's even a story about the annual chocolate hunt. Cheeky's just an expert at hiding!

Start shopping now… once you shop, you can't stop!

Here's your hidden Exclusives Shopping List! As you find each cutesie Shopkin, tick it off the list!

Pumpkinella

Curly Fries

Coco Nutty

Sponge Cake

Rolly Roll

Margarina

Hot Apple Pie

La'Lotion

MEET THE SHOPKINS!

Profile Key

👍 **Favourite hobby**

💬 **Friends would describe as...**

❤️ **Shopkins BFF**

BAKERY

CHEESE LOUISE

👍 Telling cheesy jokes to my friends!

💬 She loves to dance to cheesy songs and takes the cake when it comes to being smooth!

❤️ Queen of Tarts

PATTY CAKE

👍 Speed Baking!

💬 She loves to sprinkle joy wherever she goes! 'Life's what you Bake it!'

❤️ Macca Roon

TOASTIE BREAD

👍 Taking Toasty Pops by surprise!

💬 Warm at heart with a very dry sense of humour!

❤️ Lana Banana Bread

FRUIT AND VEG

SWEET PEA

👍 Juggling!

💬 Cute and cosy, and ready to pop out of their pod!

❤️ Cherie tomato

PEACHY

👍 Chillin' out with Ice Cream Dream

💬 You get a warm fuzzy feeling when you meet her!

❤️ Ice Cream Dream

SHOES

SNEAKY SALLY

👍 Running up and down basketball courts

💬 A real sneaky mover, she's got a bouncy personality!

❤️ Kelly Jelly

JENNIFER RAYNE

👍 Splashing in puddles

💬 Always up to her ankles in trouble, she loves to splash out on her friends!

❤️ Taylor Rayne

HATS

CASPER CAP

👍 Playing baseball

💬 He can cap off any outfit and is always in peak condition!

❤️ Flappy Cap

TAYLOR RAYNE

👍 Splashing in puddles

💬 A little wet behind the ears but she'll always cover for you!

❤️ Jennifer Rayne

Profile Key

👍 Favourite hobby

💬 Friends would describe as...

❤️ Shopkins BFF

SWEET TREATS

SUZIE SUNDAE

👍 Relaxing on a Sundae

💬 A Shopkin with a lot of glass! She can whip up a yummy treat in seconds!

❤️ Kylie Cone

MACCA ROON

👍 Getting a new colour put in!

💬 A bit of an airhead but one of the sweetest Shopkins you'll meet!

❤️ Patty Cake

CANDY APPLE

👍 Playing Fiddle-sticks

💬 If she starts something, she sticks with it! She looks sweet but can be a bit sour!

❤️ PopRock

INTERNATIONAL FOOD

TACO TERRIE

👍 Dancing around Sombreros

💬 Extremely cheeky, wants to be involved with everything!

❤️ Lammy Lamington

NETTI SPAGHETTI

👍 Twirling in ballet classes

💬 A true Italian beauty, she loves to take a spin and is long and thin

❤️ Sausage Sizzle

HOMEWARES

CHATTER

👍 Talking, talking and talking!

💬 She's just desperate to get engaged and keeps looking for the perfect ring!

🖤 Mobile Mary

FROST T FRIDGE

👍 Making icy poles

💬 She's a cool chic who loves to chill out, but she can get a bit frosty!

🖤 Blow-anne and Mixie & Maxie

STATIONERY

PENNY PENCIL

👍 Writing and drawing

💬 She always has a point to make and likes to leave her mark!

🖤 Erica Eraser

ERICA ERASER

👍 Making things disappear by magic!

💬 She's a real problem solver and loves it when other Shopkins make mistakes

🖤 Penny Pencil

SECRET SALLY

👍 Playing Hide and Secret

💬 Trustworthy and faithful, she'll keep all your secrets forever

🖤 Noni Notebook

SEASON 3

TICK OFF YOUR COLLECTED SHOPKINS™ TO SEE WHICH ONES YOU STILL HAVE TO FIND!

COLLECT THEM ALL!

○ COMMON
● RARE
● ULTRA RARE
● SPECIAL EDITION

FINISHES:
- CHOC FROSTED SHOPKINS™
- POLISHED PEARL SHOPKINS™
- COOL JEWELS SHOPKINS™

POLISHED PEARL SPECIAL EDITION

******* BAKERY *******

Cheese Louise 3-001 ○	Queen of Tarts 3-002 ○	Patty Cake 3-003 ○	Lana Banana Bread 3-004 ●
Toastie Bread 3-005 ○	Candy Cookie 3-006 ○	Birthday Betty 3-007 ○	Wendy Wedding Cake 3-008 ○
Nilla Slice 3-009 ○	Cheese Louise 3-010 ●	Queen of Tarts 3-011 ●	Patty Cake 3-012 ●
Lana Banana Bread 3-013 ●	Toastie Bread 3-014 ●	Candy Cookie 3-015 ●	Birthday Betty 3-016 ●
	Wendy Wedding Cake 3-017 ●	Nilla Slice 3-018 ●	

******** HATS ********

Casper Cap 3-019 ○	Hattie Hat 3-020 ○	Flappy Cap 3-021 ○	Brimmy 3-022 ●
Toni Topper 3-023 ●	Shady 3-024 ●	Bonnie Beret 3-025 ○	Taylor Rayne 3-026 ●
Casper Cap 3-027 ●	Hattie Hat 3-028 ●	Flappy Cap 3-029 ●	Brimmy 3-030 ●
Toni Topper 3-031 ●	Shady 3-032 ●	Bonnie Beret 3-033 ○	Taylor Rayne 3-034 ●

******* SHOES *******

Beverley Heels 3-035 ○	Shoes-Anne 3-036 ●	Jennifer Rayne 3-037 ●	Molly Moccasin 3-038 ●
Lizzy Lace-up 3-039 ●	Sneaky Sally 3-040 ●	Snug Ugg 3-041 ●	Wilma Wedge 3-042 ●
Beverley Heels 3-043 ●	Shoes-Anne 3-044 ●	Jennifer Rayne 3-045 ●	Molly Moccasin 3-046 ●
Lizzy Lace-up 3-047 ●	Sneaky Sally 3-048 ●	Snug Ugg 3-049 ●	Wilma Wedge 3-050 ●

***** SWEET TREATS *****

Rock 051	Cream E Cookie 3-052	Macca Roon 3-053	Chocky Box 3-054
anda afer -055	Choc Kiss 3-056	Suzie Sundae 3-057	Candy Apple 3-058
Ginger Fred 3-059	PopRock 3-060	Cream E Cookie 3-061	Macca Roon 3-062
Chocky Box 3-063	Wanda Wafer 3-064	Choc Kiss 3-065	Suzie Sundae 3-066
	Candy Apple 3-067	Ginger Fred 3-068	

**** LIMITED EDITION ****

Ruby Earring 3-137	Chelsea Charm 3-138	Ring-A-Rosie 3-139	Ticky Tock 3-140
	Brenda Brooch 3-141	Roxy Ring 3-142	

***** HOMEWARES *****

Washa 3-103	Vicky Vac 3-104	Frost T Fridge 3-105	Blow-Anne 3-106
Teenie TV 3-107	Radio Sue 3-108	Chatter 3-109	Mobile Mary 3-110
Mixie & Maxie 3-111	Washa 3-112	Vicky Vac 3-113	Frost T Fridge 3-114
Blow-Anne 3-115	Teenie TV 3-116	Radio Sue 3-117	Chatter 3-118
	Mobile Mary 3-119	Mixie & Maxie 3-120	

***** FRUIT & VEG *****

Peachy 3-069	Wild Carrot 3-070	Sweet Pea 3-071	Pee Wee Kiwi 3-072
Aspara-Gus 3-073	Super Celery 3-074	Asbury Raspberry 3-075	Cherie Tomatoe 3-076
Peachy 3-077	Wild Carrot 3-078	Sweet Pea 3-079	Pee Wee Kiwi 3-080
Aspara-Gus 3-081	Super Celery 3-082	Asbury Raspberry 3-083	Cherie Tomatoe 3-084

*** INTERNATIONAL FOOD ***

Suzie Sushi 3-085	Humpty Dumpling 3-086	Lammy Lamington 3-087	Netti Spaghetti 3-088
Croissant d'Or 3-089	Fiona Fries 3-090	Sconnie 3-091	Taco Terrie 3-092
Sausage Sizzle 3-093	Suzie Sushi 3-094	Humpty Dumpling 3-095	Lammy Lamington 3-096
Netti Spaghetti 3-097	Croissant d'Or 3-098	Fiona Fries 3-099	Sconnie 3-100
	Taco Terrie 3-101	Sausage Sizzle 3-102	

***** STATIONERY *****

Stella Stapler 3-121	Snippy 3-122	Penny Pencil 3-123	Noni Notebook 3-124
Erica Eraser 3-125	Kelly Calculator 3-126	Rita Ruler 3-127	Secret Sally 3-128
Stella Stapler 3-129	Snippy 3-130	Penny Pencil 3-131	Noni Notebook 3-132
Erica Eraser 3-133	Kelly Calculator 3-134	Rita Ruler 3-135	Secret Sally 3-136

ODD ONE OUT

Shopping in the Shopville mall is baskets of fun, everyone gets so excited. The Shopkins are so friendly that sometimes they get caught up with the wrong team. In each basket can you find the Shopkin who's the odd one out?

1. BAKERY

2. BABY

3. SHOES

4. DAIRY

BEST FRIENDS WITH GOOD SHELF LIFE!

Every Shopkin has a best friend they like to hang out with in Shopville. They make the cutest pairs and have so much fun! Penny Pencil is trying to remember who's friends with who. Can you help her draw lines to match up the BFFs? You could look for clues on the profile pages.

CHECK THEM OUT ONLINE TOO, AT SHOPKINSWORLD.COM. OR ON THE 'MEET THE SHOPKINS' PAGES!

15

SUREST SHOPKINS FRIENDS' QUIZ!

Shopkins is all about your BFFs! So how well do you know yours? Sit opposite your friend with the Shopkins Annual between you and with a pencil or glittery pink pen, that Lippy Lips would just love, answer the questions by colouring the heart by your answer.

Then check your friendship score to see if you are destined to be BFFs forever!

My friend's favourite midnight feast snack is...

Cookies ♡ Popcorn ♡ Crisps ♡ Frozen Yoghurt ♡ Ice Cream ♡

My friend's favourite hobby is...

Snow Sports ♡ Reading ♡ Singing ♡ Dancing ♡ Sports ♡

My friend's favourite nail varnish is...

Pink ♡ Purple ♡ Blue ♡ Yellow ♡ Red ♡ Silver ♡

Which type of performance would she prefer to take part in?

Rapping ♡ Comedy ♡ Singing ♡

The thing we most love to do together is...

Movies ♡ Dancing ♡

Shopping ♡ Talking ♡

The thing we most love to do together is....

Shopping ♡   Talking ♡

Movies ♡   Dancing ♡

Which type of performance would she prefer to take part in?

Rapping ♡   Comedy ♡   Singing ♡

My friend's favourite nail varnish is....

Pink ♡   Purple ♡   Blue ♡   Yellow ♡   Red ♡   Silver ♡

My friend's favourite hobby is....

Snow Sports ♡   Reading ♡   Singing ♡   Dancing ♡   Sports ♡

My friend's favourite midnight feast snack is....

Cookies ♡   Popcorn ♡   Crisps ♡   Frozen Yoghurt ♡   Ice Cream ♡

YOUR FRIENDSHIP SCORE!

0-4
Knowing your best friend really well takes time! The more time you spend together talking, the more you'll get to know each other's favourite things!

TIP: Share two secrets each!

5-7
You're great friends and get on really well but you both have other friends you like to hang out with, too.

TIP: Throw a Shopkins Swapkins Party to get your friends all together!

8-10
You really are BFFs forever! You know everything about each other and can tell what each other is thinking!

TIP: Make each other a Shopkins pillow case Shopping Bag from page 59 and head out for a day's shopping together!

REMEMBER: THIS IS JUST A GUIDE TO FRIENDSHIP. REAL FRIENDS KNOW THAT EVERY FRIENDSHIP IS AN ADVENTURE!

Pop goes the Babysitter!

Apple Blossom, Toasty Pops and Strawberry Kiss are cooing around Dum Mee Mee when Apple Blossom realises they're running out of baby supplies!

They leave Toasty Pops on babysitting duty! How will things go?

Toasty Pops watches her friends leave and turns back to find Dum Mee Mee has disappeared!

Toasty Pops pings into action and catches Dum Mee Mee just before she slips through the doors.

18

Somehow Dum Mee Mee has climbed up to the shop's bunting and it looks like she might fall at any minute.

Toasty Pops jumps onto a bag of marshmallows that shoots her up to the bunting. She gently lowers Dum Mee Mee onto the soft bag below but suddenly...

The bunting snaps and Toasty Pops swings through the Smart Mall like Tarzan and hits a bag of flour with a puff.

Covered in flour and really cross, Toasty Pops carries Dum Mee Mee back to her rattle.

Dum Mee Mee's eyes fill with water and she does what a baby does best...she cries and cries.

Dum Mee Mee throws her rattle in a tantrum which hits Toasty Pops' button and then...

POP

Toasty Pops' toast pops out of her head! Dum Mee Mee starts to laugh at silly Toasty Pop.

HEE HEE HEE HAA HAA
HEE HEE HEE HAA HAA
HEE HEE HEE HEE HAA

Apple Blossom and Strawberry Kiss return to hear Dum Mee Mee laughing.

WOW, I'VE NEVER SEEN HER LAUGH SO MUCH! YOU'LL HAVE TO BABYSIT MORE OFTEN...

CHECK YA LATER!

IT'S A FRY-UP!

Every Shopkins get-together needs some Curly Fries!
The thing Curly Fries loves about her hair is that it's crazy and curly, and now you can make it even cooler and more fun by changing it to any colour that you can think of!

Create the curliest Curly Fries you can!

22

GET IN LINE!

Shopkins love their BFFs but they work best when they're with their team, especially when it comes to beating the queues at the checkout!

There are six teams of four Shopkins hidden in this grid. Look for them up, down, forwards, backwards and even diagonally! Tick off each team as you find them.

The teams that are hiding are:

Stationery 〇   Fruit & Veg 〇   Frozen 〇

Cleaning & Laundry 〇   Sweet treats 〇   Pantry 〇

SEASON 2

MEET THE SHOPKINS!

FRUIT AND VEG

CHLOE FLOWER
- 👍 Leafing through the newspaper
- 💬 All about flower power but never 'leafs' her friends behind
- 💜 Rockin' Broc

SILLY CHILLI
- 👍 Eating VERY hot dogs
- 💬 Some say she can seem cold but she's just a bit chilli!
- 💜 Dippy Avocado

JUICY ORANGE
- 👍 Keeping juicy secrets
- 💬 Maybe a bit pushy but she's sweet on the inside!
- 💜 Sour Lemon

DIPPY AVOCADO
- 👍 Taking a dip on a hot day
- 💬 A true greenie who likes to spread himself around!
- 💜 Silly Chilli and Brenda Blenda

CORNY COB
- 👍 Doing puzzles and maizes
- 💬 He'll admit his friends think he's a bit corny!
- 💜 Poppy Corn

SWEET TREATS

ICE-CREAM DREAM
- 👍 Chilling out alone in her cone
- 💬 She's a little bit drippy but never loses her cool
- 💜 Waffle Sue

WAFFLE SUE
- 👍 Waffling on about anything
- 💬 A total chatterbox who loves to stay toasty warm, even if it means meltdown on top!
- 💜 Ice-Cream Dream

POPPY CORN
- 👍 Going to the movies
- 💬 Warm, full of surprises and bags of fun! Great to see a movie with
- 💜 Corny Cob

PAMELA PANCAKE
- 👍 Flipping out in the diving pool
- 💬 She's stacks of fun, overflowing with sweetness but never too syrupy!
- 💜 Cheery Churro

MINNIE MINTIE
- 👍 Yoga and deep breathing
- 💬 She's a breath of fresh air and always cool to be around!
- 💜 Yummy Gum

Profile Key

👍 Favourite hobby

💬 Friends would describe as...

❤️ Shopkins BFF

SHOES

BETTY BOOT

👍 Boot scootin'

💬 The wildest boot in the west, she gets her kicks riding in the saddle!

❤️ Heels

SNEAKY WEDGE

👍 Playing "Hide and Sneak"

💬 She's footloose and fancy-free and never sweats over getting a little tongue-tied

❤️ Sneaky Sue

PROMMY

👍 Kicking up her heels

💬 She's high-spirited and never flat, known for her fabulous style

❤️ Wedgy Wendy

HEELS

👍 Tap dancing

💬 Definitely no shoe-off, she's a hard worker who buckles down!

❤️ Betty Boot

BUN BUN SLIPPER

👍 Getting ready for bed

💬 A real snoozy head who's always ready for bed! She'd better hop to it!

❤️ Cute Boot

HOMEWARES

BRENDA BLENDA

👍 Mixing with her friends

💬 She likes to stir up trouble but is a whizz at blending in with the crowd

❤️ Dippy Avocado

ZAPPY MIRCOWAVE

👍 Speed reading

💬 A real fast thinker, she can get a bit impatient - don't push her buttons!

❤️ Saucy Pan

TOASTY POP

👍 Throwing parties and giving toasts

💬 He's warm and always popping up with new stuff!

❤️ Butter Cup

SIZZLES

👍 Riding on steam trains

💬 She's warm-hearted and loves to steam through her jobs each day!

❤️ Wendy Washer

LANA LAMP

👍 Reading in bed

💬 She loves light-hearted jokes and comes up with some really bright ideas

❤️ Lisa Litter

BAKERY

CARRIE CARROT CAKE

👍 Horse riding

💬 Sweet but a little nutty, she has a 24 carrot heart of gold

❤️ Pecanna Pie

SLICK BREADSTICK

👍 Lunching in a French cafe

💬 He's crusty on the outside but warm inside - it's a tall order being a breadstick!

❤️ Alpha Soup and Faster Pasta

PECANNA PIE

👍 Going to the ballet, especially 'The Nutcracker'

💬 She's a bit nutty in the head but a real sweet heart inside

❤️ Carrie Carrot Cake

MARY MERINGUE

👍 Whipping up treats

💬 Sweeeeet and fluffy, her head is always in the clouds!

❤️ Lippy Lips

FIFI FRUIT TART

👍 Catching some sun so she's just ripe

💬 She's a fruit loop who's sometimes a sweetie, sometimes sour - always tasteful though!

❤️ Shampy

PANTRY

AL FOIL

👍 Wrapping with his friends

💬 He's strong and protective and loves to shine! Gets a bit torn between his friends

❤️ Soda Pops

HONEEEY

👍 The spelling bee and catching flies

💬 She can Bee charming, she can Bee helpful but, most of all, she Bee sweet!

❤️ Lee Tea

FASTA PASTA

👍 Shooting hoops with meatballs

💬 She's a great friend to twirl around with - she's un-spaghettable!

❤️ Fi Fi Flour and Olivia Oil

CORNELL MUSTARD

👍 Solving mysteries

💬 He's hot stuff - a little squirt with big flavor who can make any hot dog a little hotter!

❤️ Bart Beans

FI FI FLOUR

👍 Creating half-baked inventions

💬 She'll help anyone in a sticky situation even though she's messy to have around!

❤️ Fasta Pasta

BABY

BABY PUFF

- 👍 Finding shapes in the clouds
- 💬 A sweet-smelling Shopkin - she's so fit she never runs out of puff!
- 💜 Nappy Dee

SIPPY SIPS

- 👍 Singing lullabies
- 💬 Never spills a secret and likes to be held tight and sealed with a kiss!
- 💜 Dum Mee Mee

DUM MEE MEE

- 👍 Rocking out with babies
- 💬 A peacekeeper, born to shop, she's no dummy when it comes to stopping tears!
- 💜 Sippy Sips

DRIBBLES

- 👍 Taking nice warm baths
- 💬 When she hears a cry for help, this little super-hero squirt can save the day!
- 💜 Ga Ga Gourmet

BABY SWIPES

- 👍 Swiping out in a wave pool
- 💬 A real clean machine, she keeps things shiny from top to bottom!
- 💜 Shampoo Sue

CLEANING & LAUNDRY

LEAFY

- 👍 Unwinding with a good magazine
- 💬 A girl who knows her rollin life, she's always flushed with success!
- 💜 Peta Plunger

WENDY WASHER

- 👍 Spin cycle classes at the gym
- 💬 A truthful, clean-living type of girl, she lays it on the line!
- 💜 Sizzles and Sarah Softner

SWEEPS

- 👍 Brushing up on her schooling
- 💬 Don't just brush past her, she'll be your friend from 'Dust till Dawn' and can handle it all!
- 💜 Molly Mops

SQUEAKY CLEAN

- 👍 Writing poetry
- 💬 Honest and clean-cut, she's in a 'glass' of her own and loves to rise and shine
- 💜 Dishy Liquid and Leafy

MOLLY MOPS

- 👍 Playing mopscotch
- 💬 Buckets of fun, she's a real hard worker and loves to clean up on a bargain!
- 💜 Sweeps

SEASON 2

✳✳✳✳✳✳ SWEET TREATS ✳✳✳✳

Poppy Corn 2-053 ○	Minnie Mintie 2-054 ●	Banana Splitty 2-055 ●	Yummy Gum 2-056 ○
Waffle Sue 2-057 ●	Ice-cream Dream 2-058 ○	Cheery Churro 2-059 ●	Pamela Pancake 2-060 ○
Poppy Corn 2-061 ○	Minnie Mintie 2-062 ○	Banana Splitty 2-063 ●	Yummy Gum 2-064 ○
Waffle Sue 2-065 ●	Ice-cream Dream 2-066 ●	Cheery Churro 2-067 ●	Pamela Pancake 2-068 ●

✳✳✳✳✳✳✳✳ BAKERY ✳✳✳✳✳✳✳✳

Slick Breadstick 2-035 ○	Mary Muffin 2-036 ●	Carrie Carrot Cake 2-037 ●	Mary Meringue 2-038 ○
Pecanna Pie 2-039 ●	Choco Lava 2-040 ●	Fifi Fruit Tart 2-041 ●	Danni Danish 2-042 ○
Cupcake Chic 2-043 ○	Slick Breadstick 2-044 ○	Mary Muffin 2-045 ●	Carrie Carrot Cake 2-046 ○
Mary Meringue 2-047 ●	Pecanna Pie 2-048 ○	Choco Lava 2-049 ●	Fifi Fruit Tart 2-050 ○
Danni Danish 2-051 ○	Cupcake Chic 2-052 ○		

✳✳✳✳✳ CLEANING & LAUNDRY ✳✳✳✳✳

Dishy Liquid 2-087 ○	Squeaky Clean 2-088 ○	Wendy Washer 2-089 ●	Bree Freshner 2-090 ○
Molly Mops 2-091 ●	Sweeps 2-092 ○	Sarah Softner 2-093 ○	Peta Plunger 2-094 ●
Leafy 2-095 ○	Dishy Liquid 2-096 ○	Squeaky Clean 2-097 ○	Wendy Washer 2-098 ○
Bree Freshner 2-099 ○	Molly Mops 2-100 ●	Sweeps 2-101 ●	Sarah Softner 2-102 ○
	Peta Plunger 2-103 ●	Leafy 2-104 ○	

✳✳✳✳✳✳✳✳ HOMEWARES ✳✳✳✳✳✳✳✳

Toasty Pop 2-017 ○	Brenda Blender 2-018 ●	Coffee Drip 2-019 ○	Saucy Pan 2-020 ●
Ma Kettle 2-021 ○	Zappy Microwave 2-022 ●	Lisa Litter 2-023 ○	Lana Lamp 2-024 ○
Sizzles 2-025 ●	Toasty Pop 2-026 ○	Brenda Blender 2-027 ○	Coffee Drip 2-028 ○
Saucy Pan 2-029 ○	Ma Kettle 2-030 ●	Zappy Microwave 2-031 ●	Lisa Litter 2-032 ○
Lana Lamp 2-033 ●	Sizzles 2-034 ●		

○ **COMMON**
● **RARE**
● **ULTRA RARE**
● **SPECIAL EDITION**

FINISHES:
✳ **CRYSTAL GLITZ SHOPKINS™**
❀ **FLUFFY BABY SHOPKINS™**
✹ **BLING SHOPKINS™**

****** FRUIT & VEG *********

Chloe Flower 2-001	Sour Lemon 2-002	Juicy Orange 2-003	Corny Cob 2-004
Garlic Rose 2-005	Boo-Hoo Onion 2-006	Dippy Avocado 2-007	Silly Chilli 2-008
Chloe Flower 2-009	Sour Lemon 2-010	Juicy Orange 2-011	Corny Cob 2-012
Garlic Rose 2-013	Boo-Hoo Onion 2-014	Dippy Avocado 2-015	Silly Chilli 2-016

********* PANTRY **********

Fi Fi Flour 2-069	Bart Beans 2-070	Fasta Pasta 2-071	Olivia Oil 2-072
Honeeey 2-073	Al Foil 2-074	Toffy Coffee 2-075	Cornell Mustard 2-076
Chris P Crackers 2-077	Fi Fi Flour 2-078	Bart Beans 2-079	Fasta Pasta 2-080
Olivia Oil 2-081	Honeeey 2-082	Al Foil 2-083	Toffy Coffee 2-084
Cornell Mustard 2-085	Chris P Crackers 2-086		

********* SHOES ***********

Prommy 2-105	Sneaky Sue 2-106	Heels 2-107	Sneaky Wedge 2-108
Betty Boot 2-109	Wedgy Wendy 2-110	Bun Bun Slipper 2-111	Cute Boot 2-112
Prommy 2-113	Sneaky Sue 2-114	Heels 2-115	Sneaky Wedge 2-116
Betty Boot 2-117	Wedgy Wendy 2-118	Bun Bun Slipper 2-119	Cute Boot 2-120

********** BABY **********

Dribbles 2-121	Ga Ga Gourmet 2-122	Dum Mee Mee 2-123	Baby Swipes 2-124
Sippy Sips 2-125	Baby Puff 2-126	Nappy Dee 2-127	Shampoo Sue 2-128
Dribbles 2-129	Ga Ga Gourmet 2-130	Dum Mee Mee 2-131	Baby Swipes 2-132
Sippy Sips 2-133	Baby Puff 2-134	Nappy Dee 2-135	Shampoo Sue 2-136

GO ON A SHOPKINS™ SPREE!

✓ TICK OFF YOUR COLLECTED SHOPKINS™ TO SEE WHICH ONES YOU STILL HAVE TO FIND!

****** LIMITED EDITION ******

Marsha Mellow 2-137	Rub-a-Glove 2-138	Lenny Lime 2-139	Lee Tea 2-140
Donna Donut 2-141	Angie Ankle Boot 2-142		

YOUR SHOPKINS SLEEPOVER!

WOW, WHAT A BRILLIANT IDEA! WAS IT YOUR IDEA TO HOST YOUR SHOPKINS SLEEPOVER? THERE'S SO MUCH EXCITEMENT IN SHOPVILLE! OF COURSE, EVERYONE WANTS TO BE ON THE VIP GUEST LIST!

You'll need snacks, games and an essential sleepover kit, so Strawberry Kiss has started a shopping list for you - she'll happily help out and round everyone up!

BERRY special

CHECK! SHOPPING LIST!

Start by choosing your top 15 must-have Shopkins from the 30 listed below, and see if you can remember which team they're in.

Put a tick in the heart next to each name so that Strawberry Kiss knows where to take her trolley!

Marsha Mellow ♡
Poppy Corn ♡
Ice-Cream Dream ♡
Lolli Poppins ♡
Cheeky Chocolate ♡
Jelly B ♡
Candy Kisses ♡
Cupcake Chic ♡
Kooky Cookie ♡
D'Lish Donut ♡
Lippy Lips ♡
Polly Polish ♡
Shampy ♡
Silky ♡
Scrubs ♡

La' Lotion ♡
Mindy Mirror ♡
Toofs ♡
Scrubs ♡
Curly Fries ♡
Gran Jam ♡
Bread Head ♡
Breaky Crunch ♡
Soda Pops ♡
Blushy Brush ♡
Wally Water ♡
Secret Sally ♡
Penny Pencil ♡
Erica Eraser ♡
Bun Bun Slipper ♡

Now, is there anything you've not seen on the shelves in Shopville? Make up five of your own Shopkins! E.g. Penny Pillow.

CHECK YOUR INVITATIONS!

Photocopy or scan the invite to duplicate and send to your friends.

DEAR

....

Shopkins

Once you shop...You can't stop!

YOU'RE INVITED TO MY SHOPKINS SLEEPOVER!

ON .... AT ....

PLEASE BRING A SLEEPING BAG AND DON'T FORGET TOOFS AND SCRUBS!

CHECK YA LATER! FROM ....

Be sure to ask an adult for help when using scissors!

Little Sweetie!

MY SLEEPOVER GAMES!

Who doesn't love a game of Shopkins Bingo, Hide and Seek or a Best Friend Quiz? Here are my two favourite games, though!

1. The Shopkins Tray Game!

Lay out around 10 Shopkins and get everyone to memorise who's on the tray. Then, whip one away and see who's the first to spot who's missing!

2. Guess Me in Ten!

Take it in turns to pick a Shopkin out of a bag (without showing who it is!) and give your friends one question each, or up to 10, to guess who you are. Remember, they must ask questions about your personality and accessories but you can only answer 'Yes' or 'No!'

CUPCAKE CHIC'S CLEVER TIPS!

You'll need some special snacks! Fancy fruit kebabs, sensational smoothies or taste-bursting tacos (there's a d'lish tacos recipe on page 58!)

SHOPVILLE HIDE AND SEEK COLOURING CHALLENGE!

The store is closed and some of the Shopkins are grabbing some Cheezey B action in the burger bar before they go on stage in the Small Mall. Can you get them all ready for the show by colouring them in? You could use glitter pens to make them shine and dazzle!

Can you find six Shopkins who like to take to centre stage and perform? There are also three Shopkins who are really shy and would rather sneak out in a trolley!

Colour in a heart every time you spot a limelight lovin' Shopkin!

There are three trolleys to take the shy Shopkins back to the shelves. Draw lines to send the right ones home!

Lover's Day

It's Lover's Day and Lippy Lips is busy getting creative with hearts, making cards with Kooky Cookie!

DON'T YOU JUST LOVE TODAY? IT JUST FILLS YOUR HEART WITH LOVE! YUP, NOTHING CAN RUIN THE MOOD I'M IN!

Just then, singing can be heard coming from below. They look through the window to see Slick Breadstick serenading Lippy Lips on the guitar.

LIPPY! OH LIPPY! YOU'RE AS BEAUTIFUL AS FRENCH TOAST... WITH LIPS AS RED AS... UM ... BEETROOTS! HA HA HA... WILL YOU BE MINE? SAY YOU'LL BE MINE!

The two curious Shopkins soon realise what's going on and are not impressed!

Strawberry Kiss is next! Just as she was hanging a string of hearts around the shelves, Slick Breadstick appears with a table for two and dinner by candlelight!

The girls all get together, they are very cross with Slick Breadstick for trying to ask them all out!

THIS NEEDS TO STOP!

I AGREE!

ERM, WHAT IF WE ASK HIM OUT?!

Lippy Lips has a plan!

HUSH...

SHHH...

All three of the Shopkins find Slick Breadstick and ask him out, covering him in kisses!

Slick realises it's time to run and the girls fall around giggling at Lippy Lips' clever game.

DANCING IN THE AISLE

The Shopkins love to party and are shaking it on down all over the store! But, their funky dancing is causing mayhem. Give these Shopkins some pizazz with your pens by colouring them in.

Cornell Mustard, who loves solving mysteries, is looking for seven letters that make up the name of a Shopkin who likes to talk!

Prommy is helping with the lost property - she's looking for the six coin purses hidden in this scene.

Circle each one as you find them!

MEET THE SHOPKINS!

PARTY FOOD

SODA POPS
- 👍 Shaking it on the dancefloor!
- 💬 She's super bubbly and sweet, and adds fizz to any party!
- ❤️ Rainbow Bite

CHEEZEY B
- 👍 Rapping with his BFFs
- 💬 He never stops rapping or rhyming!
- ❤️ Freezy Peazy and Chee Zee

FAIRY CRUMBS
- 👍 Parties!
- 💬 She's cute and colourful and loves pink and purple!
- ❤️ Soda Pops

WISHES
- 👍 Singing a tune!
- 💬 She's a real party starter but quite attention-seeking
- ❤️ Soda Pops

WOBBLES
- 👍 Hip-hop dancing
- 💬 Klutzy and a bit of a worry wart but she just can't stop jiggling!
- ❤️ Snow Crush

PRETZ-ELLE
- 👍 Gymnastics
- 💬 She's scatter-brained, cheeky & charming!
- ❤️ Sally Shakes

DAIRY

CHEE ZEE
- 👍 Rapping with his BFFs!
- 💬 A confident performer and a little bit crackers!
- ❤️ Cheezey B and Freezy Peazy

GOOGY
- 👍 Juggling
- 💬 Clumsy and shy, she needs to come out of her shell
- ❤️ Spilt Milk

SPILT MILK
- 👍 Splashing in the local pool
- 💬 A bit of klutz, she likes to stir things up!
- ❤️ Breaky Crunch

SWISS MISS
- 👍 Being a stand-up comedian
- 💬 A hilarious jokester, no way are her jokes cheesy!
- ❤️ Tommy Ketchup

FROZEN

ICE CREAM DREAM
- 👍 Igloo building
- 💬 Scoops of fun but can be a bit of a headache!
- ❤️ Cheeky Chocolate

FREEZY PEAZY
- 👍 Rapping with his BFFs
- 💬 He's super cool and the best rapper in the pod
- ❤️ Soda Pops

SNOW CRUSH
- 👍 Snowkin building and curling
- 💬 A snowkin builder extraordinaire
- ❤️ Popsi Cool

COOL CUBE
- 👍 Winter sports
- 💬 A bit of a snow bunny who hates hot weather!
- ❤️ Snow Crush

YO-CHI
- 👍 Swirling around the dancefloor
- 💬 She's well-cultured and full of variety
- ❤️ Melonie Pips

POPSI COOL
- 👍 Ice skating
- 💬 Cold outside, warm and gooey in the centre!
- ❤️ Cool Cube

BAKERY

BREAD HEAD
- 👍 Chatting on the phone
- 💬 A real chatterbox and very independent
- ❤️ Kooky Cookie

KOOKY COOKIE
- 👍 Acrobatics and reading
- 💬 She's shy, sensitive and doesn't like trying new things
- ❤️ Bread Head and Apple Blossom

MINI MUFFIN
- 👍 Going to brunch
- 💬 Sweet inside, she's an early riser and has so much energy!
- ❤️ Spilt Milk

D'LISH DONUT
- 👍 Golf and basketball
- 💬 Super sweet but competitive, too!
- ❤️ Cheeky Chocolate

Profile Key

👍 Favourite hobby

💬 Friends would describe as...

❤️ Shopkins BFF

SWEET TREATS

BUBBLES

👍 Singing a tune!

💬 She'll chew any-one's ears off but is really kind

❤️ Lolli Poppins

LOLLI POPPINS
👍 Hairdressing

💬 She loves to smile and make Shopkins laugh!

❤️ Candi Cotton

JELLY B

👍 Skipping!

💬 Full of beans and a colourful personality!

❤️ Candy Kisses

CHEEKY CHOCOLATE

👍 Pranking!

💬 She's very cheeky and is never afraid to get dirty!

❤️ D'Lish Donut and Apple Blossom

LE'QUORICE

👍 Hopscotch

💬 Vintage but the life and soul of any party!

❤️ Mandy Candy

CANDY KISSES

👍 Writing poetry

💬 Romantic and smooth but never had a date

❤️ Candi Cotton

FRUIT AND VEG

APPLE BLOSSOM
👍 Going on adventures!

💬 An adventurer, kind to the core

❤️ She has lots!

POSH PEAR
👍 Playing cards

💬 A bit spoilt but really friendly

❤️ Lippy Lips

MISS MUSHY-MOO

👍 Making mud pies

💬 A softy with a good head

❤️ Rockin' Broc

PINEAPPLE CRUSH

👍 Surfing and Sunbaking

💬 Silly and fun, and a lover of sun!

❤️ Melonie Pips

STRAWBERRY KISS

👍 Writing poetry

💬 A daydreamer, often away with the fairies

❤️ Apple Blossom

PANTRY

TOMMY KETCHUP

- 👍 Trolley Riding
- 💬 Extremely cheeky, wants to be involved with everything!
- 💜 Frank Furter

GRAN JAM

- 👍 Knitting
- 💬 Caring, gentle, she's mum to everyone
- 💜 Papa Tomato

BREAKY CRUNCH

- 👍 Working out
- 💬 Full of energy, a morning Shopkin!
- 💜 Spilt Milk

SUGAR LUMP

- 👍 Perfecting the ultimate cup of tea
- 💬 A real sweety, she's easy to be around
- 💜 Wishes

SALLY SHAKES

- 👍 Dancing the Cha-Cha
- 💬 She adds flavour to any party!
- 💜 Peppe Pepper

PEPPE PEPPER

- 👍 Shaking it on the dancefloor!
- 💬 Always sneezing, and he likes to spice things up!
- 💜 Sally Shakes

HEALTH & BEAUTY

SCRUBS

- 👍 Tubing
- 💬 Chatty and always grinning!
- 💜 Toofs

POLLY POLISH

- 👍 Shopping!
- 💬 Always trying new colours and styles
- 💜 Lippy Lips

LIPPY LIPS

- 👍 Shopping!
- 💬 A fashionista, a bit bossy!
- 💜 Apple Blossom and Polly Polish

SHAMPY

- 👍 Swimming
- 💬 We never know if she's Silky or Shampy!
- 💜 Silky

SILKY

- 👍 Swimming
- 💬 She has a great sense of style
- 💜 Shampy

SEASON 1

****** **SWEET TREATS** ******

Bubbles	Candy Kisses	Le'Quorice	Cheeky Chocolate	
1-047	1-048	1-049	1-050	

Candi Cotton	Lolli Poppins	Mandy Candy	Jelly B	
1-051	1-052	1-053	1-054	

Miss Twist	Bubbles	Candy Kisses	Le'Quorice	
1-055	1-056	1-057	1-058	

Cheeky Chocolate	Candi Cotton	Lolli Poppins	Mandy Candy	
1-059	1-060	1-061	1-062	

Jelly B	Miss Twist
1-063	1-064

TICK OFF YOUR COLLECTED SHOPKINS™ TO SEE WHICH ONES YOU STILL HAVE TO FIND!

FINISHES:
- ✨ GLITTER SHOPKINS™
- ❄ FROZEN SHOPKINS™
- ✳ METALLIC SHOPKINS™

- ⚪ COMMON
- ⚫ RARE
- ⚫ ULTRA RARE
- ⚫ SPECIAL EDITION

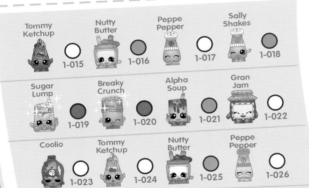

********** **PANTRY** **********

Tommy Ketchup	Nutty Butter	Peppe Pepper	Sally Shakes
1-015	1-016	1-017	1-018

Sugar Lump	Breaky Crunch	Alpha Soup	Gran Jam
1-019	1-020	1-021	1-022

Coolio	Tommy Ketchup	Nutty Butter	Peppe Pepper
1-023	1-024	1-025	1-026

Sally Shakes	Sugar Lump	Breaky Crunch	Alpha Soup
1-027	1-028	1-029	1-030

Gran Jam	Coolio
1-031	1-032

******* **FRUIT & VEG** *******

Apple Blossom	Rockin' Broc	Strawberry Kiss	Pineapple Crush
1-001	1-002	1-003	1-004

Melonie Pips	Miss Mushy-Moo	Posh Pear	Apple Blossom
1-005	1-006	1-007	1-008

Rockin' Broc	Strawberry Kiss	Pineapple Crush
1-009	1-010	1-011

Melonie Pips	Miss Mushy-Moo	Posh Pear
1-012	1-013	1-014

****** **LIMITED EDITION** ******

Cupcake Queen	Buttercup	Tin'a' Tuna	Twinky Winks
1-137	1-138	1-139	1-140

Papa Tomato	Sunny Screen
1-141	1-142

********* BAKERY *********

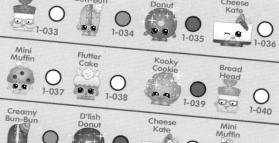

Bread Head 1-033	Creamy Bun-Bun 1-034	D'lish Donut 1-035	Cheese Kate 1-036
Mini Muffin 1-037	Flutter Cake 1-038	Kooky Cookie 1-039	Bread Head 1-040
Creamy Bun-Bun 1-041	D'lish Donut 1-042	Cheese Kate 1-043	Mini Muffin 1-044
Flutter Cake 1-045	Kooky Cookie 1-046		

********* DAIRY *********

Chee Zee 1-065	Swiss Miss 1-066	Spilt Milk 1-067	Ghurty 1-068
Millie Shake 1-069	Flava Ava 1-070	Dollops 1-071	Googy 1-072
Chee Zee 1-073	Swiss Miss 1-074	Spilt Milk 1-075	Ghurty 1-076
Millie Shake 1-077	Flava Ava 1-078	Dollops 1-079	Googy 1-080

********* FROZEN *********

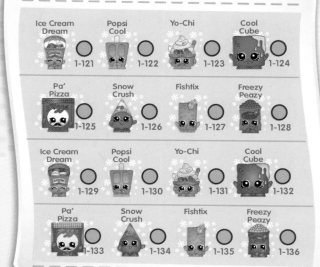

Ice Cream Dream 1-121	Popsi Cool 1-122	Yo-Chi 1-123	Cool Cube 1-124
Pa' Pizza 1-125	Snow Crush 1-126	Fishtix 1-127	Freezy Peazy 1-128
Ice Cream Dream 1-129	Popsi Cool 1-130	Yo-Chi 1-131	Cool Cube 1-132
Pa' Pizza 1-133	Snow Crush 1-134	Fishtix 1-135	Freezy Peazy 1-136

******* HEALTH & BEAUTY *******

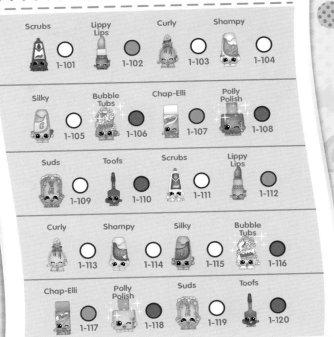

Scrubs 1-101	Lippy Lips 1-102	Curly 1-103	Shampy 1-104
Silky 1-105	Bubble Tubs 1-106	Chap-Elli 1-107	Polly Polish 1-108
Suds 1-109	Toofs 1-110	Scrubs 1-111	Lippy Lips 1-112
Curly 1-113	Shampy 1-114	Silky 1-115	Bubble Tubs 1-116
Chap-Elli 1-117	Polly Polish 1-118	Suds 1-119	Toofs 1-120

********* PARTY FOOD *********

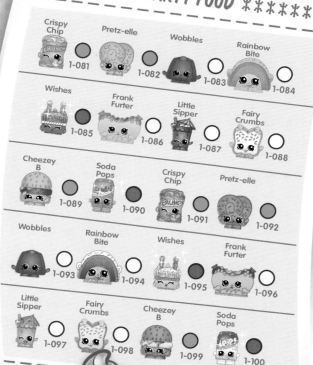

Crispy Chip 1-081	Pretz-elle 1-082	Wobbles 1-083	Rainbow Bite 1-084
Wishes 1-085	Frank Furter 1-086	Little Sipper 1-087	Fairy Crumbs 1-088
Cheezey B 1-089	Soda Pops 1-090	Crispy Chip 1-091	Pretz-elle 1-092
Wobbles 1-093	Rainbow Bite 1-094	Wishes 1-095	Frank Furter 1-096
Little Sipper 1-097	Fairy Crumbs 1-098	Cheezey B 1-099	Soda Pops 1-100

SPOT THE DIFFERENCE!

You know how those cheeky Shopkins like to play hide and seek? Look really carefully at these pictures of Cheeky Chocolate and Spilt Milk. They look the same but see if you can find the six differences. Can you find them all? Each time you find one, colour in a price tag!

WORD PUZZLE!

Write a letter in each heart shape to make two friendly Shopkins names.

POSH PEA ♡ OCKIN' BROC

SIZZLE ♡ UGAR LUMP

SAUCY PA ♡ UTTY BUTTER

GRAN JA ♡ ARY MUFFIN

SLICK BREADSTIC ♡ OOKY COOKIE

WENDY WASHE ♡ UB-A-GLOVE

46

FIGURE IT OUT!

Apple Blossom has noisy feet! When she walks, her feet make the sound of a till ringing or a chicken clucking! Someone's playing tricks! See if you can use your undercover secret shopper skills to find out who's to blame before she works it out herself!

CAN YOU FIGURE OUT WHO'S PLAYING TRICKS?

- She likes to get messy!
- Her favourite hobby is pranking her friends!

- She's never afraid to get dirty
- You'll find her in the sweet treats section

IT'S A CANDY CRUSH!

Some of the sweet little Shopkins have got themselves stuck in this jar, all crushed up! How many of each can you spot? Draw a tally chart for each Shopkin. Strawberry Kiss has got it started for you as she's keen to find her friends!

IMAGE	NAME	TALLY
	MINNIE MINTIE	IIII

Limited Edition

MEET THE SHOPKINS!

SEASON 1: *Metallic Shopkins*

CUPCAKE QUEEN

👍 Hosting grand balls

💬 She dreams about becoming royalty and loves a crown of frosting!

BUTTERCUP

👍 Loves showing off his great taste

💬 He's rich but never spoiled, and remembers being whipped into shape!

💜 Bread Head

SUNNY SCREEN

👍 A day at the beach

💬 She's a bit of a worrier but she just doesn't want anyone getting burned on her watch

TIN 'A' TUNA

👍 Swimming upstream

💬 He often thinks there's something fishy going on and loves canned applause

TWINKY WINKS

👍 Surprising her friends

💬 She says Shopkins are the cream of the crop but can sponge off her friends a bit

PAPA TOMATO

👍 Chatting with pals on the vine

💬 He's a seasoned storyteller who loves to keep hold of family heirlooms

💜 Gran Jam

THE HIDDEN EXCLUSIVE SHOPKINS ARE HIDING ON THESE PAGES...
15, 17, 22, 30, 33, 34, 43, 46

Profile Key
👍 Favourite hobby
💬 Friends would describe as...
❤️ Shopkins BFF

SEASON 2: Bling Shopkins

MARSHA MELLOW
👍 Telling stories by the campfire

💬 She's a real softie and dislikes being too hot - it makes her feel puffy!

❤️ Choco Lava

RUB-A-GLOVE
👍 Water sports

💬 She loves to dish the dirt and often asks for a hand!

❤️ Molly Mops

LENNY LIME
👍 Concentrating!

💬 She loves to dish the dirt and often asks for a hand!

❤️ Sour Lemon

LEE TEA
👍 Handbags, shoulder bags, and tea bags!

💬 He dislikes steep prices and often smells trouble brewing!

❤️ Sugar Lump

DONNA DONUT
👍 Holing up with a good book

💬 Her first memory's popping out of the oven and she loves to sing Dough-Re-Mi!

❤️ Dozens of friends!

ANGIE ANKLE BOOT
👍 Strutting about in leg warmers

💬 She takes problems in her stride and is practical, yet sleek

❤️ Cute Boot

SEASON 3: Cool Jewels Shopkins

ROXY RING
👍 Going to weddings

💬 She always has a sparkle in her eye and is a cut above the rest!

❤️ Ring-A-Rosie

RING-A-ROSIE
👍 Playing piano

💬 She loves to get attached and once she's on your finger will never let go!

❤️ Roxy Ring

TICKY TOCK
👍 Watching time go by!

💬 Takes time to get to know her but the seconds will fly by once you do!

❤️ Chelsea Charm

CHELSEA CHARM
👍 Hanging with my BFF

💬 This little charmer has a strong heart and will never break yours!

❤️ Ticky Tock

RUBY EARRING
👍 Listening to classical music

💬 A stylish earring who is lobes of fun!

❤️ Brenda Brooch

BRENDA BROOCH
👍 Dinner parties with friends

💬 Likes to be worn out but she always shines to the occasion!

❤️ Ruby Earring

LIMITED EDITION HUNT!

The Shopkins love to have fun and are preparing for a trolley dash. They want to pick up all of their Limited Edition friends in the fastest time possible! Kooky Cookie is upstairs in the office, calling out instructions over the loud speaker!

From what she can see, can you tell her which grid square they will find each of the Limited Edition Shopkins? There's also a Shopkin hiding somewhere in the store - who is it? Work out the clues at the bottom of the page and fill in the coordinates.

Read the numbers across horizontally and then up vertically for the pair of coordinates.

	H	V
1. CUPCAKE QUEEN	3	7
2. BUTTERCUP	9	2
3. TIN' A' TUNA	(..... , ...)
4. TWINKY WINKS	(..... , ...)
5. PAPA TOMATO	(..... , ...)
6. SUNNY-SCREEN	(..... , ...)
7. MARSHA MELLOW	(..... , ...)
8. RUB-A-GLOVE	(..... , ...)
9. LENNY LIME	(..... , ...)

	H	V
10. LEE TEA	(..... , ...)
11. DONNA DONUT	(..... , ...)
12. ANGIE ANKLE BOOT	(..... , ...)
13. ROXY RING	(..... , ...)
14. RING-A-ROSIE	(..... , ...)
15. TICKY TOCK	(..... , ...)
16. CHELSEA CHARM	(..... , ...)
17. RUBY EARRING	(..... , ...)
18. BRENDA BROOCH	(..... , ...)

Okay, so you've found all of the cute little Limited Edition Shopkins, now you just need to find the sneaky Shopkin hiding in the store. Take the horizontal grid number from Melonie Pips and add 2 to it, then take the vertical grid number from Lee Tea and add 2 to it.

⤷ +2   ⤷ +2

Melonie Pips (...... , ...) Lee Tea (...... , ...) = (...... , ...)

Who is the hidden Shopkin? _ _ _ _ _   _ _ _ _ _ _ _

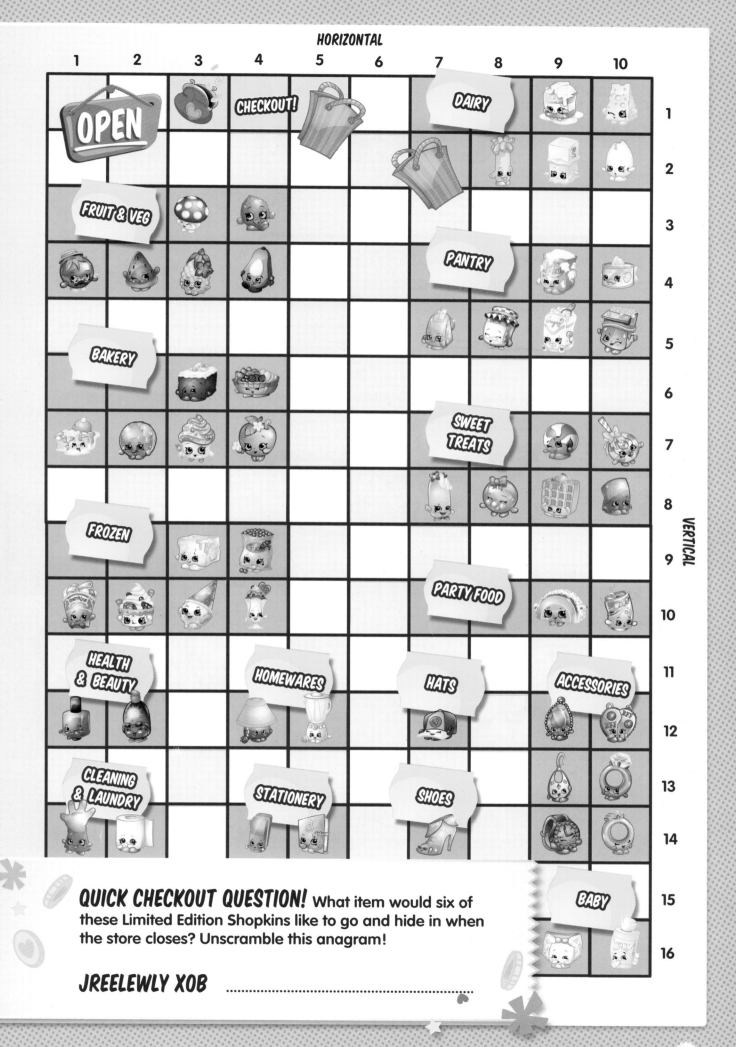

HORIZONTAL

1 2 3 4 5 6 7 8 9 10

OPEN

CHECKOUT!

DAIRY

FRUIT & VEG

PANTRY

BAKERY

SWEET TREATS

FROZEN

PARTY FOOD

HEALTH & BEAUTY

HOMEWARES

HATS

ACCESSORIES

CLEANING & LAUNDRY

STATIONERY

SHOES

VERTICAL 1–16

BABY

QUICK CHECKOUT QUESTION! What item would six of these Limited Edition Shopkins like to go and hide in when the store closes? Unscramble this anagram!

JREELEWLY XOB ....

51

The Big Cheeky Hunt

Who will find Cheeky Chocolate and win the grand prize in the annual chocolate hunt?

Apple Blossom and Cheeky Chocolate are up on stage, and Apple Blossom is going through the rules for the chocolate hunt!

CHEEKY WILL HIDE SOMEWHERE IN THE STORE AND THE FIRST SHOPKIN TO FIND HER WINS THEIR CHOICE OF EITHER THE BUNNY PLUSHY OR THE NEW CAR!

IF WE FAIL TO FIND CHEEKY, THE PRIZE GOES TO HER!

But Kooky Cookie isn't going anywhere in a hurry by the looks of it!

Strawberry Kiss and Lippy Lips are bragging about their cunning plan to team up and beat Cheeky! But who is hiding in the shelves as they walk past?

WITH US WORKING TOGETHER WE SHOULD DOUBLE THE CHANCE OF WINNING!

YUP! NOTHING CAN ESCAPE OUR GAZE!

Slick Breadstick is checking the health and beauty aisles and stops in his tracks as he sees himself in the mirror.

HERE MON CHERIE! I WILL NOT LET YOU ESCAPE ME! NOTHING CAN ESCAPE MY KEEN SENSE OF...

SACRE BLEU! WHO IS THIS HANDSOME FELLOW! HOH HOH HOH!

Apple Blossom is in the security booth looking for Cheeky.

The Shopkins stop in horror as they hear screams from Cheeky.

The kind and caring Apple Blossom rushes to the scene!

CHEEKY, ARE YOU OKAY?

YES! JUST GET HER OFF ME! SHE'S SO HEAVY!

Cheeky didn't think any one would still be at the starting line...

Kooky makes a run for the Bunny and snuggles up!

YOU WON KOOKY! PICK YOUR PRIZE!

AT LEAST...MAYBE I CAN BORROW THE CAR?

B-B-BUT... THE CAR!

CHECK YA LATER!

JUST GET THE JEWELS

Help Kooky Cookie find her way to the Shopville Jewellery Box, collecting six pieces of precious jewellery on her way.

Draw a line to show the path Kooky needs to follow to collect those jewels in the correct order. Make a note of the letters that she picks up along the way.

START HERE

Congratulations...you found all the jewels!

Kooky has reached the jewellery box, but there's still a code to crack before she can open it!

Spell out the word that the letters make up.

P R O M M Y

TAKE SOME TACOS!

TACO TERRIE IS NEW ON THE SCENE IN SHOPVILLE AND HE'S SO EXCITED TO SHARE SOME OF HIS FAVOURITE FILLINGS... WHETHER YOU'RE GETTING CREATIVE IN THE KITCHEN FOR YOUR FAMILY OR BECAUSE YOU'RE HOSTING A SHOPKINS SWAPKINS CLUB MEETING, THERE'S A TASTY TACO RECIPE FOR EVERYONE. HERE ARE THREE FILLINGS TO GET YOU STARTED!

ALL YOU NEED IS:

- 3 or 4 corn tortilla tacos
- 200g chopped up meat of your choice - pre-cooked roasted chicken, gently fried beef or spaghetti bolognese mix.
- Chopped up vegetables such as tomatoes, peppers, red onions and avocado. Replace with your favourites!
- 150g grated cheese
- One packet of tomato salsa
- Sour cream dip or dressing
- Half a lime

HOW TO MAKE THEM:

- Take 3 or 4 crisp corn tortilla taco shells.
- Filling 1: Ask a grown-up to help you gently fry some minced beef with chopped up red onions, tomatoes and peppers. Pack the tortillas with the warm mixture and pop a garnish of parsley on top. Taco Terrie does like to go to town on toppings, so sprinkle some grated cheese over the top and he'll be your friend forever!
- Filling 2: Ask your grown-up to bring a cooked chicken home, and help you to chop up chunks of the meat to mix with some avocado slices, some salsa and again, top with cheese. Dippy Avocado and Taco Terrie are great friends. For an extra fun twist, squeeze a drop of lime over the filling before you serve!
- Filling 3: If these two fillings are too exotic, just cram as much spaghetti bolognaise inside some taco shells as possible! Ask a grown-up to help with the spaghetti bolognese. It could get messy munching them but hey, Shopkins are all about having fun so you may as well join in!
- You can serve with salad and sour cream, or just nibble as they come!

PERFECT PILLOW CASE BAG FOR A SHOPKINS SPREE!

MAKE SURE YOU ASK AN ADULT FOR HELP WITH COOKING AND CUTTING!

WHEN IT COMES TO HITTING THE SMALL MALL WHAT EVERYONE NEEDS IS A SHOPPING BAG SO THAT YOU CAN TAKE YOUR COLLECTION WITH YOU WHILE YOU SHOP FOR MORE LITTLE FRIENDS! IT'S REALLY EASY TO MAKE THIS PILLOWCASE SHOPPING BAG, AND YOU CAN EVEN ADD A POCKET INSIDE TO KEEP YOUR PENNY PURSE OR LIPPY LIPS! HERE'S HOW TO TRANSFORM AN OLD PILLOW CASE INTO A PRETTY SHOPKINS SHOPPING BAG!

ALL YOU NEED IS:

- A grown-up to help you with any cutting, sewing or ironing!
- A pillow case with the pattern you want
- Scissors
- Needle and thread
- An iron, just like Sizzles!
- Velcro with a sticky back

GET CRAFTY! HERE'S WHAT TO DO!

1. Lay the pillow case out flat. Cut two identical, curved sections from the top two corners, to leave a long handle in the top - centre of the rectangle.

2. To make a sturdy handle, sew a seam across the top to join the two sides together. Ask a grown up to use an iron, just like Sizzles, to turn it over and pin a hem on the edges. Sew, then press with the iron again. Sizzles will love to get involved!

3. Use the scraps you have cut off to make extra pockets inside, to keep your Shopkins safe when you're swinging by the Small Mall. Sew the edges on inside your bag, somewhere secret, and just use a little Velcro to keep the pocket closed and safe! Once you've done that, you're all set and good to go!

59

CHECK YA LATER!

It's been so much fun getting together with you in Shopville this time, hanging out with our BFFs and meeting the Shopkins. Did you meet anyone new? Who's now top of your list to collect or try and meet at a Shopkins Swapkins club meeting?

Don't you think the fluffy Baby Shopkins are just tooooooo cute? Dum Mee Mee is going to keep everyone on their toes with her crazy games though, and Apple Blossom and Strawberry Kiss now think Toasty Pops is the best babysitter in Shopville! Uh oh!

You must have some fab ideas now about creating your own Shopville at home, so make your shopping list and pillow case shopping bags and swing into store soon. Get your hands on as many of the new Shopkins as possible, 'coz remember, once you shop, you can't stop!

ANSWERS

PAGE 14: ODD ONE OUT
1. Bakery - Honeeey
2. Baby - Pumpkinella
3. Shoes - Dippy Avocado
4. Dairy - La'Lotion

PAGE 15: BEST FRIENDS WITH GOOD SHELF LIFE!
Scrubs - Toofs
Cheese Louise - Queen of Tarts
Posh Pear - Lippy Lips
Pineapple Crush - Melonie Pips
Lana Banana Bread - Toastie Bread
Donna Donut - D'lish Donut
Poppy Corn - Corny Cob
Casper Cap - Flippy Cap

PAGE 23: GET IN LINE

PAGE 33: HIDE AND SEEK

Shy Shopkins - Googy, Kooky Cookie, Popsi Cool

Limelight lovin' Shopkins - Rockin' Broc, Cheezey B, Bubbles, Chee Zee, Wobbles and Freezy Peazy

PAGE 38: STORE DETECTIVE IN SHOPVILLE!

Cornell Mustard spelled out CHATTER

PAGE 46: SPOT THE DIFFERENCE

WORD PUZZLE!
Posh Pea (R) ockin' Broc
Sizzle (S) ugar Lump
Saucy Pa (N) utty Butter
Gran Ja (M) ary Muffin
Slick Breadstic (K) ooky Cookie
Wendy Washe (R) ub-a-Glove

PAGE 47: FIGURE IT OUT!
Cheeky Chocolate has been playing tricks.

IT'S A CANDY CRUSH!
Le'Quorice 5, Candy Kisses 5, Lolli Poppins 3, Jelly B 8, Bubbles 8

PAGE 50: LIMITED EDITION HUNT!
1. Cupcake Queen (3,7)
2. Buttercup (9,2)
3. Tin' a' Tuna (10,4)
4. Twinky Winks (7,8)
5. Papa Tomato (1,4)
6. Sunny-Screen (2,12)
7. Marsha Mellow (10,8)
8. Rub-a-Glove (1,14)
9. Lenny Lime (4,3)
10. Lee Tea (7,5)

11. Donna Donut (2,7)
12. Angie Ankle Boot (7,14)
13. Roxy Ring (10,13)
14. Ring-A-Rosie (10,14)
15. Ticky Tock (9,14)
16. Chelsea Charm (10,4)
17. Ruby Earring (9,13)
18. Brenda Brooch (9,12)

The slippery Hidden Exclusive Shopkin is Apple Blossom (4,7)

PAGE 56: JUST GET THE JEWELS!

The name the Jewels are spelling out is PROMMY

FINISH!

Visit Pedigreebooks.com
to view our full range of titles.

Annuals

Fun Learning

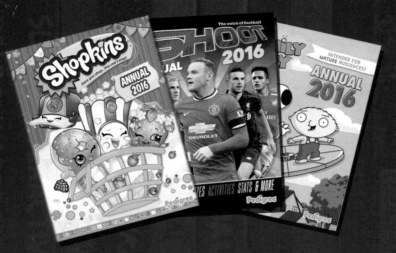

Activity Annuals

Yearbooks

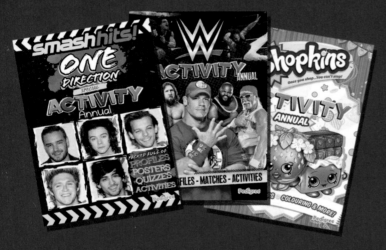

Pedigree®

THE #1 ANNUALS & YEARBOOK PUBLISHER

Pedigree Books, Beech Hill House, Walnut Gardens, Exeter EX4 4DH